**W9-AYR-727**

Cornerstones of Freedom

Presidential Elections

Miles Harvey

 CHILDRENS PRESS®
CHICAGO

Library of Congress Cataloging-in-Publication Data

Harvey, Miles.
  Presidential elections / by Miles Harvey.
    p. cm.—(Cornerstones of freedom)
Includes index.
  Summary: Examines how presidential elections have changed over
the past 200 years, discussing topics such as primaries, national
conventions, television campaigns, and funding.
  ISBN 0-516-06629-3
  1. Presidents—United States—Election—Juvenile literature.
[Presidents—Elections. 2. Elections. 3. Politics, Practical.] I. Title.
II. Series.
JK524.H374 1995
324.6'3'0973—dc20
                                                        95-1560
                                                          CIP
                                                          AC

In 1787, politicians from around the United States gathered in Philadelphia, Pennsylvania. Their job was to write a constitution, the basic set of ground rules under which their young nation would operate. This gathering was called the Constitutional Convention.

One of the delegates at the convention was a man from Pennsylvania named James Wilson. On June 1, 1787, Wilson said something that shocked and angered some of his fellow delegates. He proposed that one person should be given certain executive responsibilities in the new U.S. government. This person would be called a "president."

James Wilson

George Washington speaks at the Constitutional Convention.

Why were the other politicians upset with this idea? Because between 1775 and 1781, America had fought the Revolutionary War to get rid of a powerful leader, Britain's King George III. Now Americans wanted a government in which no single person had as much power as a king. This kind of government is called a "republic." In a republic, many people help run the country.

But between the end of the Revolutionary War and the Constitutional Convention, too many people had been running the United States. The first plan for U.S. government was known as the Articles of Confederation. The Articles— which went into effect in 1781— gave the most power to the individual states. Each state made its own laws without consulting its neighbors or the national government. This system led to many fights between states. And it caused another big problem: nobody had enough power to take action on issues that affected the nation as a whole.

James Wilson and others argued that a president could help solve these problems. After much debate, most of the delegates at the Constitutional Convention agreed. And they

King George III of England

figured out a way to ensure that the president could never obtain too much power. They divided the government into three parts, known as branches. These three branches are still the main components of our government today:

- The *legislative branch* is known as Congress, and is comprised of elected representatives in the House of Representatives and the Senate. The legislative branch is responsible for making the nation's laws.

- The *judicial branch* consists of the court system, and is headed by the Supreme Court. The judicial branch is in charge of interpreting the nation's laws.

- The *executive branch* is run by the president (also called the "chief executive"), and is responsible for carrying out the nation's laws.

By dividing the government into these three different parts, the delegates to the Constitutional Convention made sure that the United States would remain a republic. But they wanted to do even more to guarantee that the president would not be as powerful as a king. They decided that, unlike a king, the president would be chosen by the nation's citizens through elections. This system of citizens electing their leaders is called a "democracy."

Before they left Philadelphia, the delegates made several other decisions about the president. All of these rules were written into the U.S. Constitution. They decided that there would also be a vice president who would take over the presidency if the president died or left office. An election would be held every four years to elect the president and vice president. A president must be at least thirty-five years old, must be a natural-born citizen of the United States, and must have lived in the United States for at least fourteen years. In the 1780s, this meant that only a wealthy white man could be president. That's because women, African Americans, Native Americans, and many poor people were not considered full citizens.

Signing the United States Constitution

The U.S. Constitution was finally passed into law on June 21, 1788. It was now time for the country's first presidential election to take place. There was never much doubt that George Washington would be elected as the nation's first president. He was a military hero of the American Revolution, and he was known to virtually every American.

George Washington takes the oath of office as the first president of the United States.

Unlike today's presidential candidates, Washington did not have to seek endorsements from other politicians, hire a huge staff of campaign workers, or shake hand with thousands of voters. He did not buy advertisements, grant interviews to journalists, or debate his opponents. In fact, Washington did not even have any opponents!

HOW A PRESIDENT IS ELECTED

The system of electing a president has changed in many ways since George Washington's first election in 1789. For modern presidential candidates to make it to the White House, they don't have to win just one election—they have to win four!

1. Presidential Caucuses and Primaries

These two kinds of elections allow members of the major political parties (Republicans and Democrats) to help choose their party's presidential candidate. Some states hold "caucuses." In this type of election, big groups of party members gather in meeting halls to vote for candidates. At left, Iowa voters caucus at a local fire station. Most states, however, use "primary elections." In primaries, each voter goes out and votes individually for a party candidate. The different states hold caucuses and primaries over several months, beginning in the winter and ending in the spring.

2. Presidential Nominating Conventions

In the summer before the November election, the Democrats and Republicans hold separate conventions. Most delegates at these conventions are chosen based on how well the candidates they support performed in caucuses and primaries. Delegates vote to decide officially who will be the party's candidate in the general election.

3. General Election (Popular Election)

This election takes place on the Tuesday after the first Monday of November. A presidential election is held every four years.

Voters in all states go to polling places to cast their votes. The ballot lists Republican and Democratic candidates as well as those from smaller political parties and other, independent candidates.

4. Electoral College

Even after a candidate wins the general election, he is not officially president until he wins in the Electoral College. The Electoral College gives final, official approval of the people's choice in the general election.

Members of the Electoral College represent individual states. In most states, the presidential candidate who wins the general election gets all of that state's electoral votes. Even if a candidate loses a state by a tiny margin of the popular vote, he or she gets no electoral votes from that state. The number of Electoral College votes a state receives is based on how many representatives and senators the state has in Congress. And the number of congressional representatives a state has is based on its population. So in a presidential election, it is vital for a candidate to win the general election in states with large populations, such as New York and California—these states have the most electoral votes.

John Adams

Alexander Hamilton

After serving one four-year term as president, George Washington was reelected in 1792. Again, nobody ran against him in the election. This was the last U.S. election that had only one presidential candidate.

By the time George Washington retired in 1796, American political leaders had divided into two distinct groups, called "parties." These parties disagreed about how the government should be run. The Democratic-Republicans, led by Thomas Jefferson, wanted the states to have a lot of control. They did not want the national government (especially the president) to gain too much power. The Federalists, led by John Adams and Alexander Hamilton, believed a strong national government was vital to the country's stability and economy. These first two U.S. political parties have long since disappeared. Nonetheless, Americans still disagree about how much power the national government should hold.

The fighting between these two parties continued for years. After George Washington retired from office, John Adams defeated Thomas Jefferson in the 1796 election. In 1800, Adams was up for reelection. He lost the race to Jefferson. There was a problem, however, with this election.

The Constitution stated that after all electoral votes were counted, the candidate with a majority became president, and the second-place finisher became vice president. When the electoral votes were counted in 1800, Thomas Jefferson and Aaron Burr ended up in a tie. Burr was the vice-presidential candidate from Jefferson's own party. A tie meant that the House of Representatives would decide the election, with each state casting one vote.

Thomas Jefferson

Many Federalists were still angry that their candidate, Adams, had lost the election. So when the vote came to the House, some Federalists voted for Burr, instead of Jefferson, to stand in the way of the Democratic-Republicans' victory. Over the next week, the House debated the matter, and they voted thirty-five more times before a majority vote was reached. Finally, Jefferson was elected president, and Burr was elected vice president.

Aaron Burr

In 1804, the Constitution was amended to avoid such problems. The Twelfth Amendment states that members of the Electoral College must vote separately for president and vice president. This means that it is impossible for a presidential candidate to lose an election to his own vice-presidential running mate.

John Quincy Adams

Andrew Jackson

The 1824 election was disrupted by another problem with the Electoral College system. The Constitution requires that to become president, a candidate must win more than half of the votes in the Electoral College. In 1824, four candidates ran—but none ended up with a majority of electoral votes. There were 261 electoral votes cast, so one candidate needed at least 131 votes to win. Andrew Jackson finished first with ninety-nine votes—more than any other candidate, but not enough for victory. Thus, the legislative branch again was called upon to choose a winner. Congress elected John Quincy Adams, the second-place finisher in the original vote. A bitter Andrew Jackson said, "The people have been cheated." It was hard to argue with him.

Jackson did not give up on his dream of becoming president. In 1825, he helped form a new political organization that later became the Democratic Party. Jackson and his new party ran against Adams in 1828. By that year, many states had eased laws that prevented men from voting if they did not own property or pay enough taxes. Because of these reforms and other changes to the election system, there were three times as many voters in 1828 as there were in 1824. That was a big help to Jackson, who was a war hero and was very popular among average Americans. Jackson defeated Adams by a huge margin to become the seventh president of the United States.

On the day that Jackson took office, huge crowds of well-wishers gathered in the nation's capital to see their hero. They even made their way into a party at the White House! Andrew Jackson's vast popularity proved to other politicians that they must appeal to ordinary citizens as well as to rich people.

Andrew Jackson won the presidency because he was so popular with ordinary citizens. He even opened up the White House to these citizens for his inauguration party. Unfortunately, the White House sustained minor damage from the rowdy party.

This trend toward democracy also influenced the political parties. In the past, a party's presidential candidate had been selected in private by a small group of powerful politicians. But beginning in 1832, all the parties began holding nominating conventions. At these conventions, a large number of party members gathered and decided who would be their party's presidential candidate.

In 1854, a new political party emerged on the scene. It was called the Republican Party. Nearly a century and a half later, the Republican Party is still one of the two major parties in the United States, along with the Democratic Party.

The Republican Party was formed by politicians who were opposed to the spread of slavery in the United States. In the northern half of the country, it was illegal to own slaves. But in the southern states, millions of blacks were forced to work without pay or basic human rights. Many people in the North wanted to get rid of slavery throughout the country. Southern slave owners, however, refused to give up their slaves.

These white southerners were alarmed by the rise of the anti-slavery Republican Party. In 1856, Republican candidate John C. Fremont failed to win the presidential election. In 1860, the Republicans ran a candidate they hoped would have a better chance of winning. His name was Abraham Lincoln.

The nation was so divided over the issue of slavery that four major candidates with differing views ran for president in 1860. The Democratic Party broke into two opposing groups. The northern Democrats ran Stephen A. Douglas. The southern Democrats nominated John C. Breckinridge. Another party, the Constitutional Unionists, ran John Bell.

Abraham Lincoln eventually won the 1860 election, even though he was not listed on the ballot in southern states. The South was so opposed to Lincoln that his election led to a split in the nation. Southern states left the Union and formed their own nation, called the Confederate States of America. By 1861, the Civil War had begun between the North (the Union) and the South (the Confederacy).

As the election of 1864 approached, the war was going badly for the North. Many northerners were blaming Lincoln for the long and costly war that had claimed thousands of lives. Even Lincoln doubted he could beat his Democratic opponent, General George B. McClellan.

An 1860 Republican campaign poster for Abraham Lincoln (left) and vice-presidential candidate Hannibal Hamlin (right)

But just weeks before the election, the North began scoring important military victories. This helped Lincoln. He also gained popularity by choosing a Democrat, Andrew Johnson, as his running mate. Lincoln wound up defeating McClellan in 1864 by a solid margin.

At least 540,000 Americans lost their lives in the Civil War. When it was over, the North had won, and the southern slaves were eventually freed. On April 14, 1865, just five days after the South's surrender, President Lincoln was shot in the head by an assassin. But Lincoln's death did not halt the cause of African-American rights. In 1870, the Fifteenth Amendment to the Constitution was ratified. This amendment gave African-American men the right to vote in elections.

The assassination of President Lincoln: on April 14, 1865, John Wilkes Booth crept up behind Abraham Lincoln at Ford's Theatre in Washington, D.C., and then shot Lincoln in the head.

The 1876 presidential race between Republican Rutherford B. Hayes and Democrat Samuel Tilden was one of the most controversial in U.S. history. The outcome of this close race depended on the results in three key southern states. But the Democrats and Republicans each accused the other of cheating in those states. In the end, Congress assigned a special commission to count the votes and decide who would be the next president. The commission, controlled by Republicans, determined that Hayes had won. To this day, many historians disagree with the commission's findings. They say that Tilden was the actual winner.

Hayes and the Republicans were right about one thing. They said that southern whites used intimidation to keep African-American voters from casting their ballots. This was an undeniable fact. In some cases, the ballots cast by blacks were actually changed by white officials. Some polling places were secretly moved so that black voters could not find them. And houses of many blacks were burned to frighten them from voting. And conditions got much worse for African Americans in the South. By the 1890s, southern states required all voters to pay special voting taxes or to pass reading tests. White politicians knew that many poor and uneducated blacks could not meet these requirements. Therefore, they could not vote. Voting rights would not improve for African Americans in the South until the 1960s.

In the early 1900s, two reforms made U.S. presidential elections significantly more democratic. First, some states began holding primary elections. Primaries give citizens direct influence on who will be their party's presidential candidate. In the decades to come, primaries became a key part of the election process. The other important reform was the Nineteenth Amendment to the Constitution, which was ratified in 1920. This amendment gave women the right to vote. For the first time in U.S. history, a true majority of all adult citizens possessed voting rights.

Technology also began changing presidential elections. In 1920, commercial radio stations began broadcasting in the United States. Candidates quickly discovered that radio was a way of reaching millions of voters at a time.

Women celebrate the passage of the Nineteenth Amendment to the Constitution in 1920. The amendment gave women the right to vote. On the balcony is women's voting-rights activist Alice Paul.

This early-1900s photograph captures presidential candidate Theodore Roosevelt on a "whistle-stop tour." Before airplane travel, some candidates would crisscross the nation by train. Stopping in every town and city along the way, they would speak to local citizens from the rear car of the train.

Until this time, most American voters never saw or heard presidential candidates speak. People learned about candidates' ideas and beliefs by reading newspapers or flyers. But with the dawn of the radio era, voters could hear candidates for the first time. Now voters were swayed not only by the candidates' political beliefs, but also by their ability to give a good speech. Calvin Coolidge won the 1924 presidential election, and he attributed some of his success to a simple fact. He said, "I have a good radio voice." And in 1928, many radio listeners were irritated by Democrat Alfred E. Smith's heavy New York accent. Republican Herbert Hoover won the election.

Calvin Coolidge

One Democrat was helped by the 1928 election—Franklin Delano Roosevelt. At the Democratic Convention, Roosevelt gave a rousing speech in favor of Smith. The speech was broadcast to a national radio audience. Listeners loved Roosevelt's smooth, deep voice and confident style. The speech helped thrust Roosevelt into the national spotlight. In 1932, Roosevelt's amazing radio skills helped him defeat Hoover and win the presidency.

Roosevelt defeated Republican Thomas E. Dewey in the 1944 election. It was Roosevelt's fourth consecutive victory in a presidential election. No other president has served more than two terms. Roosevelt's long stay in the White House prompted new fears that presidents had gained too much power in government. So in 1951, the Twenty-Second Amendment was ratified, limiting presidents to two terms in office.

In his four-term presidency, Franklin D. Roosevelt regularly spoke to the nation on radio "fireside chats." Roosevelt's radio voice was so comforting and friendly that listeners felt as though the president was sitting in their own homes by the fireside.

During this period, public-opinion polling became an important part of presidential elections. A poll attempts to predict which candidate is winning an election. This helps candidates plan their campaign strategies before the election takes place. In a poll of the public's opinion, hundreds or thousands of citizens are chosen at random to be interviewed. There are millions of voters in the United States. But by collecting and examining the opinions of just a few thousand people, polls can usually predict how the entire country will vote. In 1948, however, the polls were dead wrong. That presidential race pitted Democratic president Harry S. Truman and Republican Thomas E. Dewey. Right up until election day, opinion polls predicted that Dewey would win. On the day after the election, the *Chicago Tribune* ran a front-page headline proclaiming, "Dewey Defeats Truman." But Truman had the last laugh. When all the votes were counted, he had won reelection.

Harry Truman gets the last laugh on the pollsters in 1948. Here, he holds up the headline that incorrectly proclaimed his defeat in the presidential election.

In 1960, television became as influential in presidential elections as radio had a half-century earlier. On September 26, 1960, Republican candidate Richard Nixon debated Democrat John F. Kennedy in front of a television audience of seventy million people. It was the first televised debate between major presidential candidates. On television, Nixon looked tired and tense. Under the hot television lights, perspiration appeared on his upper lip. By contrast, the handsome Kennedy looked confident and relaxed. Historians agree that Nixon's poor television appearance was an important factor in Kennedy's eventual election victory.

In a 1960 presidential debate, television viewers were impressed by the calm and cool John F. Kennedy (right, seated), while the perspiring Richard Nixon (above) seemed nervous and worried.

Television was changing American politics in other ways. In the early 1960s, television news reports gave Americans a shocking look at the plight of southern blacks, who had been denied their political rights for centuries. These reports helped bring about the Twenty-Fourth Amendment in 1964 and the Voting Rights Act in 1965. Both of these measures greatly increased the number of African Americans who were able to vote.

After decades of struggle, African Americans now enjoy equal voting rights with all other Americans.

In 1968, Republican Richard M. Nixon was elected president. When he ran for reelection in 1972, however, several men linked to his campaign were arrested breaking into the Democratic Party headquarters at the Watergate apartment complex in Washington. Nixon won the 1972 election. But in the two years that followed, congressional investigators proved that Nixon had tried to hide his administration's close connections to the break-in. On August 9, 1974, Nixon resigned as president rather than be impeached by Congress and removed from office.

As a result of the Watergate scandal, many Americans grew mistrustful of the president, and of government in general. In 1976, Americans elected Democrat Jimmy Carter, who had been unknown in national politics before launching his campaign. He won the election by promoting himself as an "outsider"—someone who had no ties to the scandals in the nation's capital.

In 1980, Carter was defeated by another "outsider," a Republican named Ronald Reagan. Reagan was formerly a famous Hollywood movie actor, and he knew how to perform in front of television cameras. One observer called Reagan "the greatest television candidate in history." He was reelected in 1984.

Other candidates have followed Reagan's example. In 1992, Democratic candidate Bill Clinton made several television appearances that were unusual for a politician. In one television interview, he and his wife, Hillary Rodham Clinton, talked about how they had solved past problems in their marriage. On a late-night entertainment program, Clinton put on sunglasses and played the saxophone. He also hosted "town hall" discussion programs on MTV to appeal to young voters. These appearances made Clinton seem like an ordinary person, and helped him defeat his two opponents, Republican president George Bush and independent candidate H. Ross Perot.

In 1992, Bill Clinton appealed to young voters by holding "town hall" meetings on MTV.

Before television, Americans did not have direct access to presidential campaigns. In the 1800s, for instance, crowds would gather in city intersections to read election results from large billboards (below); today, millions of viewers can see events such as presidential conventions (left) on television. And airplane travel has allowed modern candidates to meet countless voters in a campaign. Ronald Reagan (bottom right) and George Bush (bottom left) were two 1980s candidates who won the White House by getting out and mingling with American citizens.

Television has played an increasingly important role in recent elections, but some critics feel that its impact is mostly negative. They say that television stresses style over substance in presidential campaigns. According to these critics, the candidates who win elections in the late twentieth century are the ones with attractive smiles and clever slogans. Candidates with good ideas might never win if they appear physically unattractive on television.

A 1992 presidential debate between George Bush (left), H. Ross Perot (center), and Bill Clinton (right).

Another problem with television concerns money. Because candidates must spend millions of dollars to produce and broadcast television commercials, presidential campaigns have become very expensive. In the 1988 election, candidates spent $500 million. In the 1992 race, presidential campaign spending was up to $550 million.

How do candidates pay for their high-priced campaigns? That's an important question. Some of the money comes through voluntary donations from regular citizens. But a lot of money comes from political action committees, more commonly known as "PACs." These PACs represent both small political groups and huge, powerful corporations. By law, PACs are allowed to give more money to candidates than individuals can. But these PACs expect something in return. When a presidential candidate wins an election, the president often pays back the PAC with political favors. Many people believe that the system of campaign financing must be changed. The millions of dollars contributed by PACs make the individual voter feel insignificant.

Presidential elections have changed tremendously since George Washington was elected in 1789 without making a single campaign speech. More than a century after Washington, 1896 Democratic candidate Williams Jennings Bryan traveled 18,000 miles by train and made more than six hundred speeches in his bid for the presidency. Even though he lost the election, Bryan's campaign style caught on. Today, all presidential candidates travel to every corner of the country to meet voters. Because they travel by airplane, their schedules are even more hectic than Bryan's. Traveling by train, Bryan could visit one or two cities in a day. Flying on a chartered jet, modern candidates can make speeches in more than a half-dozen cities and towns a day!

A well-known image from presidential campaigns—the candidate (Jimmy Carter) holding a baby

Because candidates can meet and speak to more voters, presidential elections have become more democratic than they were in the 1700s. Voters can learn more about the candidates' views, and can therefore make educated decisions about whom to vote for. And changes in society and voting-rights laws have also made elections more democratic. Now, millions of average citizens, African Americans, Native Americans, and women have won the right to vote. And in 1971, the Twenty-Sixth Amendment lowered the voting age from twenty-one to eighteen. This allowed millions more young people to participate in choosing a president.

Still, even though most adult Americans have the right to vote, not many of them actually vote. In recent presidential elections, only about half of the eligible voters cast their ballots. Tens of millions of Americans stay home every election.

And despite the fact that women and ethnic minorities are able to vote, every president of the United States has been a white male. True, the Democratic Party nominated New York congresswoman Geraldine Ferraro as its vice-presidential candidate in 1984. (Ferraro and presidential running mate Walter Mondale lost to Ronald Reagan and George Bush that year.) And in the 1988 Democratic primary election, Jesse Jackson, an African-American candidate,

finished second with 6.7 million votes. Jackson and Ferraro came closer than any other non-white, non-male Americans to winning a presidential election.

Geraldine Ferraro (left) and Jesse Jackson (right)

The U.S. system of electing a president is far from perfect. But the fact that the system has survived for more than two hundred years is proof that it is both flexible and strong. The system adapts to a changing world. But in principle, the presidential election process remains the same as it was spelled out in the Constitution. Elections are still at the center of what Abraham Lincoln called "a government of the people, by the people, for the people."

GLOSSARY

amendment – an addition that is added to a bill, law, or to the Constitution

caucus – a type of election similar to a primary election

convention – a meeting at which delegates cast votes on candidates or issues; the U.S. Constitution was written at the Constitutional Convention, and modern political parties nominate their presidential candidates at national conventions every four years

Constitutional Convention

delegate – a person chosen to express the opinions of a larger group of people

democracy – a political system in which the people choose their leaders through elections; the United States is a democracy

Electoral College – a group of people chosen by the public to elect the president and vice president; the votes of the Electoral College are based on the results of the general election

general election (or **popular election**) – the November election in which U.S. voters cast their ballots for presidential candidates

impeach – to charge a government official (such as the president) with a crime, intending to remove him or her from office

political party – a group of politicians and voters who share similar views; the Democratic Party and the Republican Party have been the two major U.S. parties since the mid-1800s

polling place – a school, church, or other public building where people come to vote in an election

Polling Place

primary election – state-by-state election in which members of the major political parties vote on who will be their party's presidential candidate

republic – a government ruled by more than one person, rather than a single ruler

TIMELINE

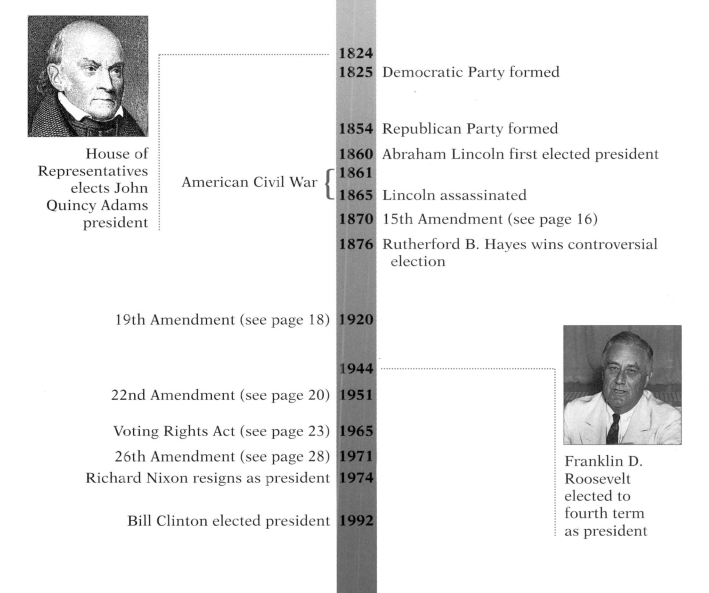

Articles of Confederation in effect **1781**

U.S. Constitution written **1787**
U.S. Constitution ratified **1788**
George Washington first elected president **1789**

1824
1825 Democratic Party formed

1854 Republican Party formed
1860 Abraham Lincoln first elected president

House of
Representatives
elects John
Quincy Adams
president

American Civil War { **1861**
1865 Lincoln assassinated
1870 15th Amendment (see page 16)
1876 Rutherford B. Hayes wins controversial
election

19th Amendment (see page 18) **1920**

1944

22nd Amendment (see page 20) **1951**

Voting Rights Act (see page 23) **1965**
26th Amendment (see page 28) **1971**
Richard Nixon resigns as president **1974**

Bill Clinton elected president **1992**

Franklin D.
Roosevelt
elected to
fourth term
as president

DEDICATION

This book is dedicated to Becca, Donna, Jack, Kali, Maggie, Katheryn, Rachel, Esther, Sean, and Milo
— future voters...and perhaps future presidents.

INDEX (*Boldface* page numbers indicate illustrations.)

PHOTO CREDITS

STAFF

Project Editor: Mark Friedman
Design & Electronic Composition: TJS Design
Photo Editor: Jan Izzo
Cornerstones of Freedom Logo: David Cunningham

ABOUT THE AUTHOR

Miles Harvey is an editor and journalist who has worked for *In These Times* and United Press International. He has also been a staff member on one presidential campaign and has volunteered on several others. He holds a bachelor's degree in journalism from the University of Illinois and a master's degree in English from the University of Michigan.

Mr. Harvey is the author of several books for Childrens Press, including the Cornerstones of Freedom title, *The Fall of the Soviet Union,* as well as biographies of Barry Bonds, Hakeem Olajuwon, and Juan Gonzalez. Mr. Harvey lives in Chicago with his wife, Rengin.